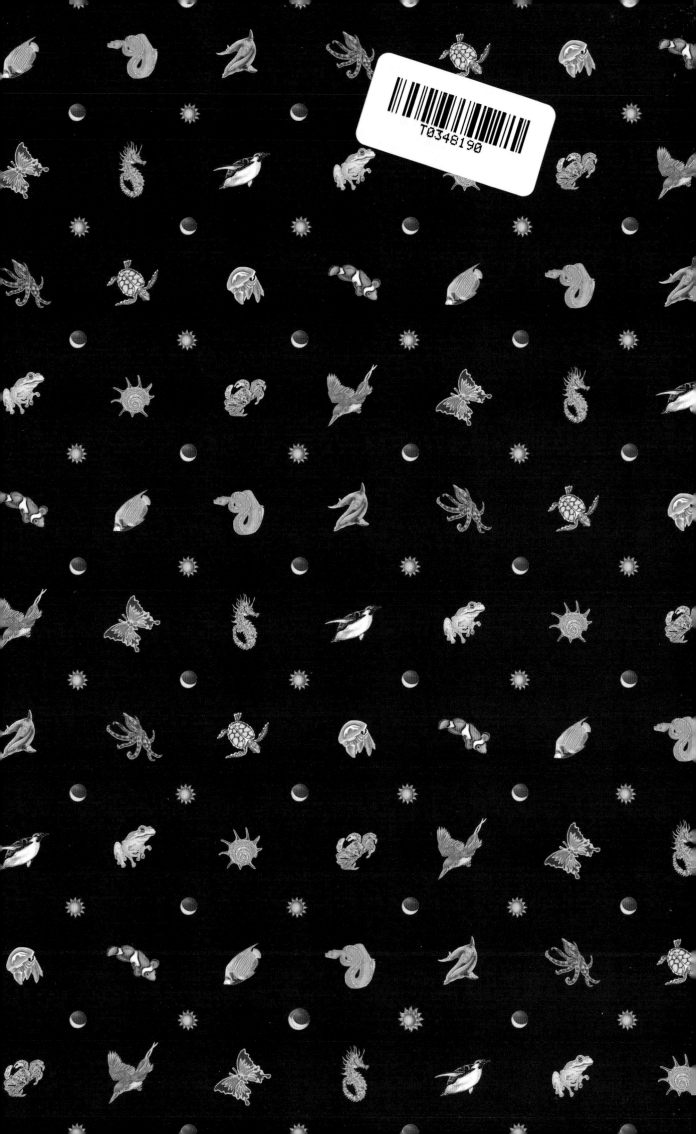

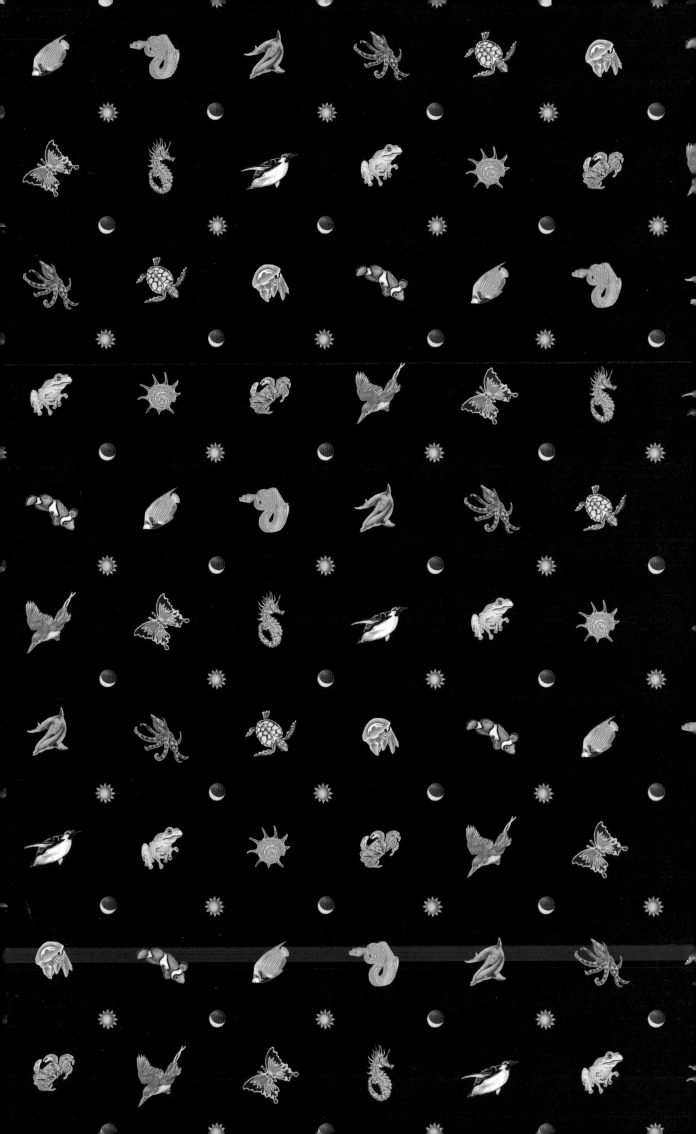

PERFECT PLANET PIE

INGREDIENTS

Rich chocolate earth
Crystallised minerals
2 clouds full of rain
Mixed seedlings
Assorted animals
A pinch of butterflies
A splash of frangipani fragrance
White fluffy clouds
Wind
A big blue ocean
1 pod of whales
1 pod of dolphins
Dozen lime green jellyfish
4 tasty turtles
3 school of fish
2 bony seahorses
1 giant orange octopus
Multi-coloured coral
Fresh green seaweed
A blend of shells and crabs
Freshwater
Powder white snow
Polar bears
Penguins
1 fat juicy walrus
Sparkling stars
A sliver of moonlight
A good dose of sunshine

METHOD

Put on your apron
and explore this book.
For *now* it is time
To become a good cook!

This book is dedicated to
Mother Nature and my daughter Casey Elle.
May they both have happy, healthy futures.

First published 2012 by SILKIM BOOKS
PO Box 693 Ballina New South Wales 2478 Australia

© Kim Michelle Toft — text and illustrations

www.kimtoft.com.au

Designed by Kim Michelle Toft
Graphic design and layout by Peter Evans
Printed by Everbest Printing Co. Ltd. China

Cataloguing in Publication Data
National Library of Australia

Author:	Toft, Kim Michelle
Title:	Recipe for perfect planet pie / Kim Michelle Toft.
ISBN:	978 0 9758390 8 9 (hbk.)
	978 0 9758390 9 6 (pbk.)
Subjects:	Sustainability--Juvenile fiction
Dewey Number:	A823.4

Kim Michelle Toft's books reflect her love of nature and the importance of
its preservation. The unique illustrations are hand drawn with gold gutta,
directly onto white silk, then painted with brushes using silk dyes.

Kim has spent her entire adult life on a beach somewhere in Australia.
She currently lives on a picturesque beach in Northern New South Wales.

Recipe

FOR
PERFECT
PLANET
PIE

KIM MICHELLE TOFT

silkim
BOOKS

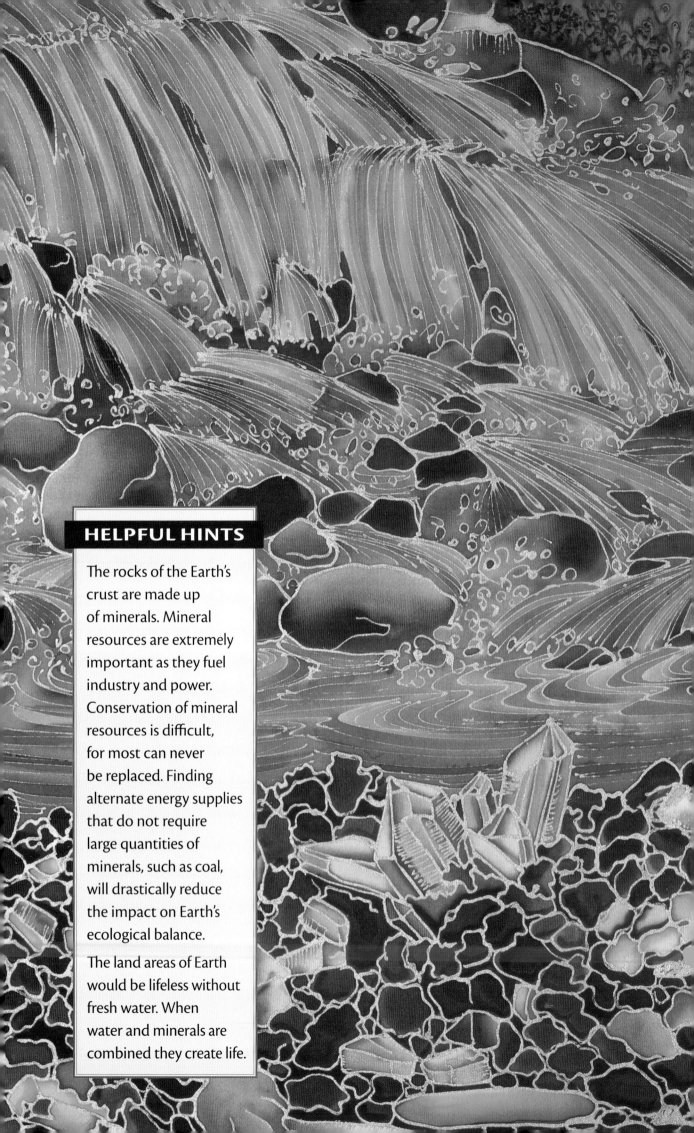

HELPFUL HINTS

The rocks of the Earth's crust are made up of minerals. Mineral resources are extremely important as they fuel industry and power. Conservation of mineral resources is difficult, for most can never be replaced. Finding alternate energy supplies that do not require large quantities of minerals, such as coal, will drastically reduce the impact on Earth's ecological balance.

The land areas of Earth would be lifeless without fresh water. When water and minerals are combined they create life.

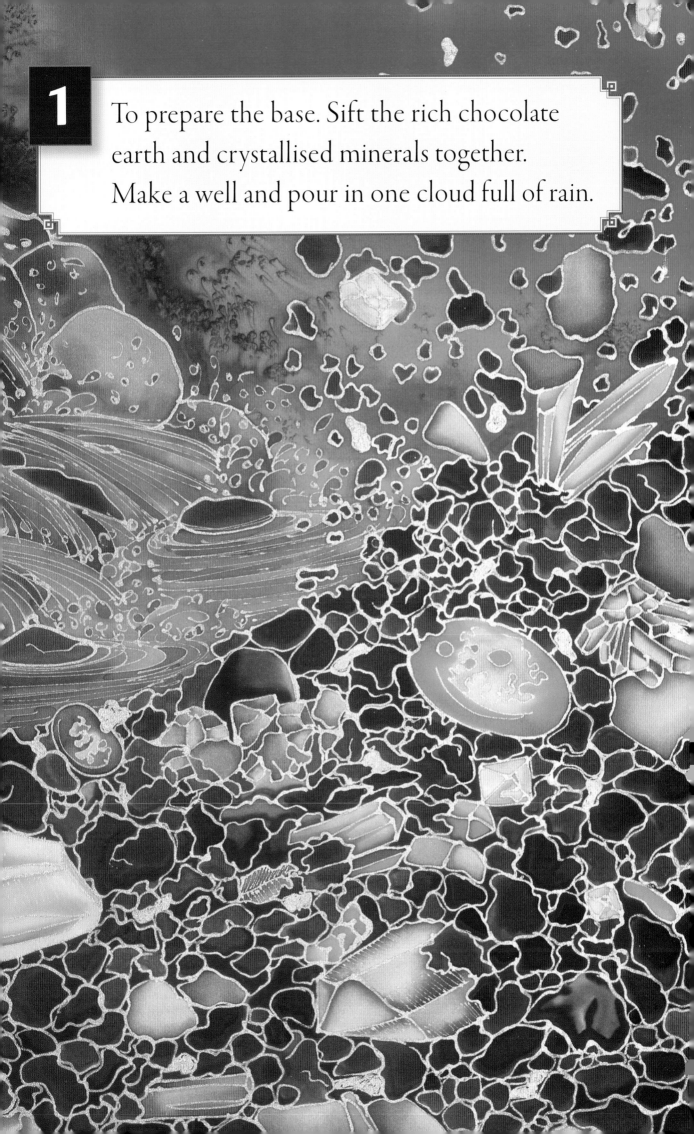

1 To prepare the base. Sift the rich chocolate earth and crystallised minerals together. Make a well and pour in one cloud full of rain.

HELPFUL HINTS

Without plants there would be no life on Earth. Plants, trees in particular, maintain the balance of gases in the atmosphere; their roots hold the soil in place and they suck up water from the ground and release it back into the air via their leaves. Plants are an excellent filtration system for the planet.

Water is vital for plant growth. About half of the material in trees is water. Water containing dissolved minerals is sucked from the soil through tiny root hairs and circulates around the plant.

2 Dot seedlings along the edge of the well and sprinkle with another cloud full of rain.

HELPFUL HINTS

The natural balance between plants and animals and their surroundings is frequently upset by the activities of people.

The destruction of forests is causing severe ecological problems, as well as the extinction of thousands of different types of wildlife. To help stop the destruction we need to buy wood products from replaceable trees, use recycled paper, avoid wastage and support conservation projects such as creating and extending national parks. The most important thing we can do is plant lots and lots of trees!

3 Gently heat with a good dose of sunshine and allow to rise. Stuff with assorted animals. *For best results*, leave undisturbed.

HELPFUL HINTS

Butterflies are among the most beautiful and fascinating of all insects. Insects make up over three quarters of a million species. They do vital work, from pollinating blossoms so that new plants can grow to composting plant matter which nourishes the soil. Pollinating insects evolved alongside flowering plants to achieve the symbiotic relationship they enjoy today. Insects are also an important food source for larger animals and may even hold the key to cures for many human diseases.

4 Add a pinch of butterflies and a splash of frangipani fragrance, then set base aside.

HELPFUL HINTS

Water that evaporates from the surface of the ocean condenses to form clouds, the water falls back to the earth as rain, snow or ice. It runs off the land into rivers that carry the water back to the oceans. As temperatures rise in the atmosphere, temperatures in the ocean also rise, wind velocity increases and the planet experiences much bigger storms and hurricanes.

Research continues into the harnessing of the wind and ocean as options to be used as cleaner renewable energy sources.

5 To make the filling, whip the wind and clouds together to form white fluffy peaks. When peaks turn purple, squeeze out excess water and combine with a big blue ocean.

HELPFUL HINTS

Ocean animals and plants are linked by the way they feed on each other which creates a food chain. When the chain is broken, ocean species can become threatened. Main causes are; habitat destruction, coastal development and tourism, illegal hunting, overfishing, climate change and pollution, e.g. fertilizers from farmlands, untreated sewerage and non-degradable litter like plastics.

Less than 1 per cent of the world's oceans are now protected areas. Expanding these areas would help regenerate habitats and endangered marine species.

6

Stir in a pod of whales, a pod of dolphins, a dozen lime green jellies, 4 tasty turtles (*just cracked from their eggs*), 3 schools of fish, 2 bony seahorses, a pretzel shaped orange octopus and a large lean shark.
DO NOT remove ingredients from the mix.

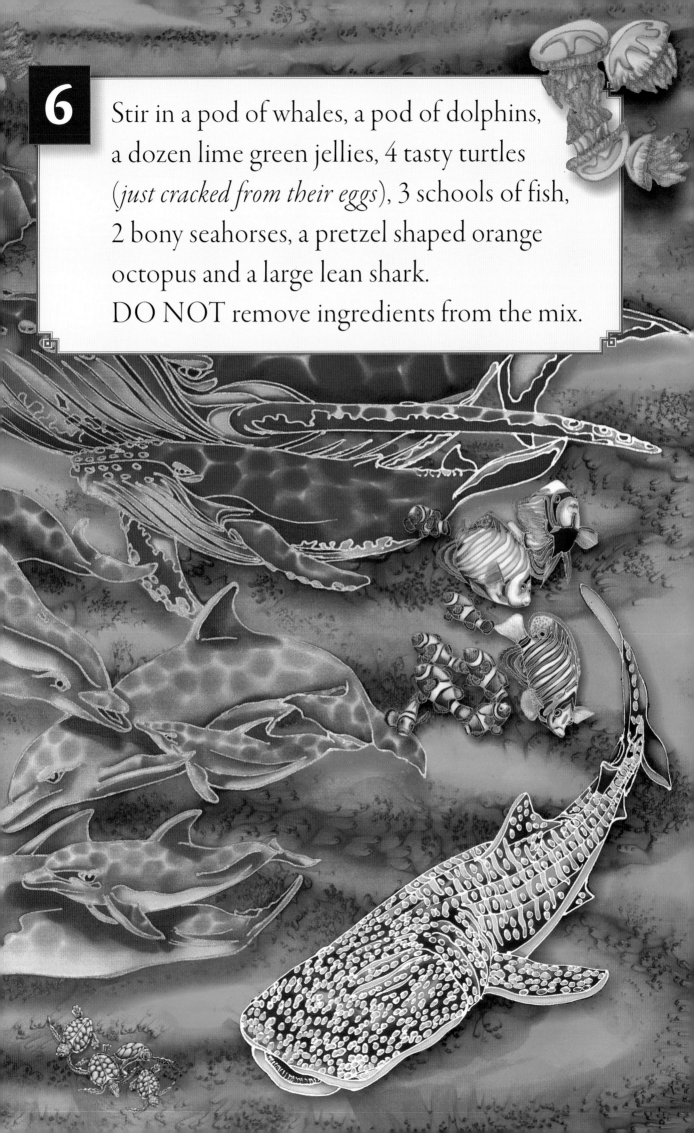

HELPFUL HINTS

Coral reefs are the most biologically diverse environments on Earth. Reefs provide food and shelter for some of the most exotic plants and animals in the world. They also protect coastlines. Reefs are easily damaged and this has a devastating effect on the lifeforms that it supports. Reefs around the world are under threat from a wide range of problems.

People as well as animals rely on coral reefs. Their immense beauty attracts tourism. When managed correctly this can actually help promote the reefs' preservation.

Creating and expanding marine sanctuaries will also help protect the reef from human impact.

7 Pour the ocean mix over the base and trim with multi-coloured coral and fresh green seaweed.

HELPFUL HINTS

The diversity of shore life reflects the dynamic and often harsh conditions found in coastal environments. Sandy beaches are formed where tides and currents deposit sand brought from rivers or weathered from rocky shores. Planting vegetation on the shoreline helps to protect the beach, by slowing down erosion caused by the waves. It also creates a habitat for wildlife.

Keeping beaches free from litter, especially plastics , is vital for a healthy ocean. Always take your rubbish away with you.

8 Continue stirring until a golden sandy crust forms around the base of the trees. Spread crust with a blend of shells and crabs.

HELPFUL HINTS

Humans throw all kinds of rubbish into the sea, but most of this rubbish never goes away. Any material thrown into the sea is potentially harmful to sea creatures. Oil and waste pollution are almost entirely due to human carelessness. It is destroying coastlines, wiping out seabird colonies and killing and contaminating marine life. To avoid polluting the oceans, we must reduce the waste we produce, recycle more and control illegal dumping. Changing dangerous waste into safer waste is also important for the health of the ocean.

9 Skim any oil and harmful lumps of rubbish from the ocean surface.

HELPFUL HINTS

Two thirds of the fresh water on the planet is locked up in ice. As water freezes, its molecules link together and form an open structure that is less dense than water, which is why ice floats.

One of the strongest signs of human induced climate change is the melting of ice. Earth's ice cover is shrinking at a faster rate than ever before. Rising temperatures is leading to rising sea levels which has led to unpredictable flooding around the world.

Creating a healthier carbon balance in the atmosphere will help address these problems.

10 Meanwhile, freeze the freshwater. When frozen, dust with soft, white, powdered snow.

HELPFUL HINTS

Polar life is essentially marine. Only a few top predators are land based. There are differences between life found at each of the poles. The Arctic or North Pole is a floating island of ice that is accessible to large land predators such as the polar bear, whereas the Antarctic or South Pole is an isolated continent that no longer has any large truly terrestrial animals. It is home to penguins and seals.

The sea ice and glaciers are rapidly melting which is having a dire impact on wildlife and is causing sea levels to rise. Cleaner energy sources equals cleaner, cooler air and in turn will help address the melting of the caps.

11 Decorate frosting with polar bears, penguins, seals and a fat juicy walrus. Keep chilled with cool, clean air.

HELPFUL HINTS

There is nothing constant in the universe. It is all ebb and flow. The Earth and the Moon are a part of the solar system, one of many planetary systems orbiting stars in the Milky Way.

The Moon is the Earth's natural satellite and our nearest neighbour in space. The Moon emits no light of its own, it simply reflects light from the Sun and so we see varying amounts of the Moon's surface lit up as it travels in its orbit.

The ocean waters are attracted toward the Moon by gravity, creating the tides.

12 Rest the pie overnight under a blanket of sparkling stars and a sliver of moonlight.

HELPFUL HINTS

The Sun is a star and dominates the solar system in size and mass and its gravity dictates the motions of the objects that orbit it. The energy that it produces drives many of the processes on the surfaces and in the atmospheres of the planets. It sustains almost all life on Earth.

Solar power is one of the most popular renewable energies currently used, however solar energy produces less than 1 per cent of the world's electricity. The demand is growing and solar is a particularly good option as a reliable energy supply.

13 Next day, bake the pie with the power of the Sun until lightly browned. Cool slightly and top with frozen caps.

14 Serve pie immediately with a side of love and a slice of happiness.

THINGS TO KNOW ABOUT PERFECT PLANET PIE

Minerals — Most rocks are a mixture of several minerals but some consist of only one, such as gold, silver or iron. Minerals are formed in many ways. Most crystallise directly from molten magna as it cools, for example, quartz which includes beautiful gems, crystals and opals. Some minerals are precipitated from water — that is, they are deposited when seas and lakes evaporate. Other minerals are formed when great heat and pressure recrystallise existing rocks

Once minerals are extracted or mined from the earth they can never be replaced. Renewable energy sources are vital for the future.

Rain — Water from the ocean is constantly being evaporated by the Sun's heat. Evaporated moisture is carried into the atmosphere as a gas called water vapour. This vapour finally forms clouds and is returned to Earth as life giving rain. Some rain water soaks into the ground, some returns quickly to the skies through evaporation, but most of it runs off the land into the sea.

Unfortunately, in heavily industrialised areas air pollutants combine together to create 'acid rain' which harms wildlife and poisons vegetation. This is another very good reason to find cleaner energy sources.

Plants — There would be no life without plants. Plants grow by making their own food from basic substances found in the soil and air by a process called photosynthesis. Photosynthesis is the way that plants produce their own nutrients, in the forms of sugars, using daylight, water and carbon dioxide. Plants also give off oxygen during this process.

Animals cannot make food, so they have to eat plants or other animals to survive.
So get busy planting!

Forestry — Forestry is important in the conservation of natural resources. In areas where the original vegetation has been destroyed, new forests are planted to prevent further soil erosion. Forest soils also absorb more rain water than exposed soil, so forests reduce the danger of flooding.

Rainforests — The value of the world's rainforests is truly immeasurable. They are vast areas of biodiversity and are critical to the health of waterways, preventing soil erosion and keeping our air clean by recycling *green house gases*. Rainforests provide basic resources such as food, medicine and fuel. Their conservation is essential in keeping a healthy balance on the planet.

Unfortunately, forests are being cleared on a massive scale. It is estimated that 2 000 trees are disappearing every minute. Pollution, the destruction of habitats and intensive farming methods all disturb the delicate balance between living things and their environment.

Animals — An animal is any living thing that is not a plant. Animals are designed to live in different habitats. Each habitat is unique because of its climate and the sorts of plants that can survive there. Plant life in specific habitats then determines what animals live there. To maintain the enormous variety of animals that currently exist, we need to conserve forest areas, keep oceans clean and create nature reserves to help protect animals, especially endangered animals.

Insects — Insects belong to the large phylum of the animal kingdom called arthropods and they are therefore related to crabs and spiders. Adult insects have a body divided into 3 parts — the head, the thorax and the abdomen. They also have 3 pairs of legs and most have one pair of feelers or antennae. Insects are the most successful class of animals, maybe a little too successful. As the temperatures rise, seasons change and insects are expanding their territories, which is actually causing and spreading disease at a much faster rate.

Flowers — Flowers are found only in the most advanced group of plants — the angiosperms. Only female plants produce seeds. Seeds cannot be produced until the flower is pollinated. Pollen is carried from the stamens to the carpels, this is usually done by wind or insects.

Wind — The Sun's heat and the spinning of the Earth cause our winds. Winds are possible because the atmosphere is made up of gases. The molecules of gases are free to move in all directions. Groups of large wind turbines, called wind farms can be built in the oceans near the shore or on large windswept plains.

Clouds — Clouds are masses of water droplets or ice crystals that are visible in the atmosphere. All air contains water vapour which is formed by evaporation from the sea, lakes and rivers. Warm air can hold more vapour than cold air. As air rises it cools, its capacity to hold water vapour decreases and eventually falls as rain.

Water — Water is a liquid and in its pure state is transparent, tasteless and odourless. Water is something many of us take for granted, but it is our most precious natural resource. Storage of freshwater and using water wisely is important to help meet the ever-growing demand. Without freshwater there would be no life on Earth.

Oceans — Oceans are complex environments covering 71 per cent of the Earth's surface which vividly sets Earth apart from other planets circling the Sun. Life abounds in the water. Huge current systems transfer heat and chemicals around the Earth, affecting the weather both over the oceans and on the land. To avoid polluting the oceans, it is important to reduce the waste we produce, recycle more, control illegal dumping of waste and change dangerous waste into safer waste.

Rainbows — Rainbows are caused by drops of water which break up sunlight into its different colours. Each drop acts as a tiny prism. A rainbow is seen in the sky directly opposite the observer. If there is a double rainbow, the second rainbow has the colours in reverse order!

Lightning — Lightning consists of huge sparks of electricity. The thunder that follows lightning is caused by the violent and sudden expansion of the air which is heated by the lightning.

Coral Reefs — Reefs are the largest geographical structures on the planet that have been formed by living organisms. They are made up of billions and billions of dead, stony coral skeletons. New polyps grow on the dead coral and the reef then grows and expands. Coral reefs face many dangers from pollution, over-exploitation and changing climatic conditions.

The impact of *global warming* on the ocean is most visible in the bleaching of the reefs (dying due to stress). Addressing rising temperatures still remains one of our greatest challenges.

Seaweed — Seaweeds are large green, brown and red algae. Seaweeds are called 'holdfasts'. They hold tight to the rock to provide anchorage. Some seaweeds on rocky shores must withstand the battering of waves, but benefits from the increased oxygen in the water and the nutrients the surf stirs up. Some seaweed can only live where there is strong wave action.

Coastlines — The world's coastlines are shaped by the immense power of waves and currents. Wave action continually moves the sand. The sea and its shores are ever-changing. Shores can range from towering, vertical cliffs to mudflats, all shaped by the immense power of tides and wave-action. The margins of the sea are one of the most diverse and challenging habitats on the planet.

Shells — Shells are the protective cases of a group of soft bodied creatures called molluscs. There are more than 100 000 different kinds of living molluscs.

Crabs — Crabs belong to a group of crustaceans called decapods, which means 'ten legs'. They have a hard case, called a carapace, which is their skeleton.

Pollution — Pollution is the contamination of the air, land, river, lakes and sea with harmful materials resulting from man's activities. Pollutants range from household garbage and sewerage to the waste materials of factories and fumes from cars.

Every year 20 billion tonnes of pollution is dumped into the oceans. Much of these are chemicals that are very dangerous for sea life. Disposing of waste responsibly should always be a number one priority.

Snow — Most rain begins as snow that melts before leaving the cloud. However, if the temperature under the cloud is below about 4° C or 39° F, precipitation falls as snow. If the ground below is freezing, the snow will settle.

Polar Regions — Both Polar regions are cold because the tilt of Earth's axis means that they receive little sunshine. Already large chunks of the Antarctic ice sheet are breaking off and sea levels are rising. And in the Arctic, ice is simply melting and disappearing.

Global warming, which is causing the sea ice to melt more quickly, has shortened the hunting season for most polar animals. Polar bears in particular are at risk of becoming extinct. They need the sea ice to hunt for seals. Polar bears are good swimmers but they risk exhaustion and drowning, having to swim long distances to reach smaller and smaller areas of ice.

Stars — Stars are spheres of glowing gas. They produce light and heat by nuclear reactions which occur inside them. An average sized star is about a million miles in diameter. The Sun is a typical star.

Moon — The Moon revolves around the Earth, from west to east, completing the trip in approximately 28 days. The Moon also controls the tides .When the Moon is overhead, the waters bulge out toward it and there is a similar occurance on the opposite side of the Earth. At its highest, the bulge is known as high tide along the shores and low tide comes when the Moon is at the horizon.

Sun — The Sun is a typical star and similar to all stars which are made of gases. Like all bodies in the universe, the Sun is in constant motion. The Sun lies 93 million miles away from the Earth and is the centre of our solar system. Without the Sun's light and heat, life could not exist on Earth. The Sun also exerts some pull on the waters, though not as much as the Moon.

Global Warming is a rapid rise in the average temperature of the whole planet as a result of the greenhouse effect. The greenhouse effect is the process by which certain gases in the Earth's atmosphere trap some of the heat given off by the Earth, keeping the planet warm enough for life to survive. Without greenhouse gases, the Earth's average temperature would be −18° C or −0.4° F, too cold for life.

Greenhouse gases include water vapour, carbon dioxide, methane, nitrous oxide, CFC's and ozone. However, over time the balance has shifted and most scientists think that deforestation and pollution have increased the amounts of greenhouse gases (especially carbon dioxide) in the atmosphere, causing the planet to warm up faster than it would naturally. Global warming is causing problems such as rising sea levels, flooding, droughts, fires, extreme weather, coral bleaching and the spread of diseases such as malaria.

To fight the effects of global warming, we need to reduce greenhouse gases by using less energy, recycling as much as possible, planting trees and developing more sources of renewable energy such as wave, tidal, wind and solar power.

"The power of positive thinking and action should never be underestimated. It is important to focus on what we do want, instead of what we don't want. And I'm sure what we do all want, is a happy, healthy planet. To save the planet, the human species will need to communicate and co-operate globally like never before. We do have the power to make change and create our own perfect planet pie. Happy cooking!".

Kim Michelle Toft

HOW TO MAKE
YOUR OWN PERFECT PLANET PIE

- Turn off lights when not in use and use energy-saving bulbs

- Avoid using the car for short journeys — walk, ride a bike, use public transport or car pool

- Support the development of more energy efficient cars and trucks

- Plant as many native trees and plants as you can, in your backyard, park, patio or rooftop

- Be water wise by fixing leaking taps and taking shorter showers. Install water tanks

- Water the garden early morning or evening to minimise evaporation and use clean waste water for plants

- Use ½ flush toilets wherever possible

- Recycle rubbish and avoid using plastic packaging

- Don't collect coral specimens or buy products made of coral

- Support local and international conservation organisations

- Read other environmentally 'healthy' books such as: *One Less Fish*, *Neptune's Nursery*, *A Sea of Words*, *The World That We Want*, *The 12 Underwater Days of Christmas* and *Tick Tock, Tick Tock, What's Up Croc?*

Planet Earth is our only home and it is up to us to create change and put our knowledge into action.

Remember: Reduce, re-use, recycle, revegetate!